Dear Family,

What's the best way to help your child love reading?

Find good books like this one to share—and read together!

Here are some tips.

• **Take a "picture walk."** Look at all the pictures before you read. Talk about what you see.

• **Take turns.** Read to your child. Ham it up! Use different voices for different characters, and read with feeling! Then listen as your child reads to you, or explains the story in his or her own words.

• **Point out words as you read.** Help your child notice how letters and sounds go together. Point out unusual or difficult words that your child might not know. Talk about those words and what they mean.

• **Ask questions.** Stop to ask questions as you read. For example: "What do you think will happen next?" "How would you feel if that happened to you?"

• **Read every day.** Good stories are worth reading more than once! Read signs, labels, and even cereal boxes with your child. Visit the library to take out more books. And look for other JUST FOR YOU! BOOKS you and your child can share!

The Editors

For Tink—Ms. Attitude.
Who loves you, Baby?
—DDB

To my son, E. Jason, and my daughter, Erin Jean,
with all my love.
—BJPD

Text copyright © 2004 by Derrick D. Barnes.
Illustrations copyright © 2004 by Barbara Jean Phillips-Duke.
Produced for Scholastic by COLOR-BRIDGE BOOKS, LLC, Brooklyn, NY
All rights reserved. Published by SCHOLASTIC INC.
JUST FOR YOU! is a trademark of Scholastic Inc.

Library of Congress Cataloging-in-Publication Data

Barnes, Derrick D.
    Stop, drop, and chill / by Derrick D. Barnes ; illustrated by
Barbara Jean Phillips-Duke.
        p. cm.—(Just for you! Level 2)
    Summary: Rhyming words help a grade-schooler deal with his angry feelings
in a more constructive way.
    ISBN 0-439-56870-6
    [1. Anger—Fiction. 2. Schools—Fiction. 3. Stories in rhyme.] I. Duke,
Barbara (Barbara J.) ill. II. Title. III Series.
PZ8.3.B25217St 2004
[E]—dc22   2004004767

10 9 8 7   11 12 13/0
        Printed in the U.S.A. 40 • First Scholastic Printing, April 2004

Stop, Drop, and Chill

by Derrick D. Barnes

Illustrated by
Barbara Jean Phillips-Duke

JUST FOR YOU!™
Level 2

Man, I used to get so mad
I'd almost blow a fuse!

I'd turn into a rocket ship
and fly out of my shoes!

When kids at school got on my nerves,
I'd be real quick to shout.

I'd make a frown, ball up my fists,
and let my temper out!

But now I've learned to mellow out.
It's just not worth the trouble.

I take my anger, shut it down,
and pop it like a bubble.

The other day at school I thought
that I would lose my mind.
Trouble seemed to hunt me down.
I'm not too hard to find.

Jamal LaBreeze sat in my seat
and took my best eraser.

Shontell O'Dell?
She pinched my arm!
She wanted me to chase her.

Deon Dumane—he's such a pain!
He bumped me in my head.

Then Tootie Teeter tripped me!
Y'all, my eyes were turning red!

Lee-Lee took my place in line
and didn't even ask.

Jo-Jo called me ugly.
She said, "Go put on a mask!"

Salina So stood up in class
and lied to all the world.

She said I was her sweet valentine,
and she was my main girl!

Wendy Woo—that girl's a mess.
She always starts a drama….

She thinks her jokes are funny.
(Don't tell jokes about my momma!)

Big Mongo took my chocolate milk.
My cookies tasted dry.

"FOOD FIGHT!" yelled the Booker Boys.
I got meatloaf in my eye.

By this time I'm about to burst—
as mad as I could be!
I could have snapped at all those kids,
but that was Angry Me.

The New Me knows that
I'll get nowhere
yelling back and fighting.

Being in trouble…
always mad—
they sure don't sound exciting.

I've learned to STOP and think about
the moves I need to make.

I DROP my anger like it's hot—
no time for big mistakes!

And like a Popsicle, I CHILL—
calm down in no time flat.

Get out of line, or act the fool?
I'm just too cool for that.

You heard—
I'm just too cool for that!

STOP, DROP, and CHILL, y'all!

▲▲▲▲▲▲ JUST FOR YOU ▲▲▲▲▲

Here are some fun things for you to do.

How Cool Are YOU?

The boy in this story uses rhymes to tell about how he feels!

Think about a time when YOU had to chill.

Draw a picture to show what happened.

Write a rhyme for your picture that tells how cool YOU are.

What else, besides a Popsicle, could you use to tell about YOUR feelings? ▲

Use some cold, cold words to tell how you chill!

▲ Some cold, cold things: ice cubes, snow man, refrigerator, air conditioner

YOUR Cool Rules

The boy who tells this story is cool.
Some of the other kids have BIG problems!

What if YOU were the principal of this school?

What would you say to the Booker Boys?

What rules would YOU make to keep kids from hitting, name-calling, and taking other people's things?

Make a list of YOUR rules!
Talk about them with your friends.

▲▲▲▲TOGETHER TIME ▲▲▲▲

Make some time to share ideas about the story with your young reader! Here are some activities you can try. There are no right or wrong answers!

Talk About It: Ask your child, "What would have happened to the boy if he had fought with everyone who bothered him?" Tell your child about a time when you stayed cool after someone did something to make you angry or hurt your feelings. Talk about a time when your child decided to chill instead of fighting.

Think About It: Read about Derrick D. Barnes on page 32. Ask your child, "Why do you think the author wrote this story? Do you think reading this book would help someone you know who gets into fights? Do you think it might change his or her style? Why?"

Read It Again: Rhyme and rhythm make this story fun to read aloud. Take turns reading it with your child. You can each read every other page. Then read the last page together, y'all!

Meet the Author

DERRICK D. BARNES says, "When kids in school are learning about fire safety, they memorize a phrase: 'STOP, DROP, AND ROLL!' When a new variation popped into my head, it seemed like a good way to help kids learn how to control their anger. That's how this story got started. I'm an expert on being cool, and keeping my cool! The truth is—I've never had a *real* fight in my life. Now how cool is that?"

Derrick is a native of Kansas City, Missouri, but he spent a good part of his early years in Mississippi. He is a graduate of Jackson State University, where he earned his degree in Marketing. He has been a copywriter for Hallmark Cards, and he had a brief career as an advice columnist for a newspaper. He lives in New Orleans, Louisiana, with his wife, Tinka, and their son Ezra. *The Low-Down, Bad-Day Blues* is another book he has written in the JUST FOR YOU! series.

Meet the Artist

BARBARA JEAN PHILLIPS-DUKE says, "I have loved to draw since I was a little girl, but I didn't start painting until I was 17 years old, and I didn't start to illustrate children's books until my own kids were almost teenagers. I love what I do, and because I have a full-time job, most of my illustration work happens early in the morning or late at night."

Barbara is a native New Yorker who was raised in the great neighborhood of Harlem in the 1960s. A self-taught painter, her artwork is filled with images of the people she sees around her every day. Barbara took classes at both City College and the Art Students League. She works at the Brooklyn Museum of Art and paints at home in Brooklyn, where she lives with her husband and two children. Other books she has illustrated include *Digby* by Barbara Shook Hazen, *What in the World* by Eve Merriam, and *F is for Flag* by Wendy Cheyette Lewison.